THE UNITED STATES OF AMERICA

PURPOSEFUL MONEY

A BEGINNER'S STEP-BY-STEP GUIDE

TO

TAKING CONTROL OF MONEY

By

Jackie Humphrey

COPYRIGHT

Jackie Humphrey
mohyfive@gmail.com
Subject line: Copyright permission

DISCLAIMER: This work reflects the experiences of the author. No liability is assumed for losses or damages due to use of the information provided. You are responsible for your own choices, actions, and results.

DEDICATION

This book is dedicated to everyone who has ever tried to overcome financial hardship. The struggle is real. The victory is sweet.

ACKNOWLEDGEMENTS

Thank you, Richard Galione of Jacksonville, Florida. This journey would never have started without your help and support way back when. We owe you a big debt of gratitude for having the courage to tell us we were doing it wrong.

Thank you to my kids, who are forever teaching me new things.

Thank you, Keith, for trusting me with our finances.

Thank you, God, the great I AM, for the financial miracles that You've pulled off, for providing our every need, and for giving us the ability to help others.

TABLE OF CONTENTS

I DON'T NEED A BUDGET!

You don't need a budget? I can't tell you how many times I've heard people say those very words.

I've heard it from doctors who had well-established, lucrative practices; from couples who have two incomes; from single moms or dads working to pay child support; from retirees who want to travel but can't afford it; from college students whose parents are footing the school bill. I've heard it from people in all stages and walks of life.

Many of them think they have enough money to spend as they please without the need to set limits, and that budgets are for those not as well off. Others believe they don't earn enough to make budgeting worthwhile. Still others assume that a budget won't work with variable income.

Yet, again and again, I hear stories of money constraints keeping people stressed, or from saving for retirement, or from taking a day trip, or helping someone in need. Seventy-three percent of Americans rank their finances as the number one stress in life, according to Capital One's December 2019 CreditWise survey[1].

Everyone uses money in some form. Some need a budget to survive, but everyone can benefit from following a budget, even if the only benefit is reducing stress. Nearly all folks have money concerns. In many situations, money controls choices. It also dashes hopes and stomps on their dreams. There are solutions, though. Everyone can benefit from a budget.

Who Am I?

I'm Jackie Humphrey. I have been a tax preparer for over 12 years and currently hold Enrolled Agent credentials with IRS. I earned my Business Management degree from Western Governors University at age 65.

In the 1980s, my Navy husband was stationed in Mayport, Florida. I was a stay-at-home mom and we had four young mouths to feed. Money was always very tight. We were regularly asking for help from family and friends. Then a financial advisor from our church taught a class on budgeting.

It changed our lives.

I learned enough to open a successful business, teaching folks how to meet their financial goals. Through this business, Family Budget Consultants, I taught groups and individuals how to get control of money. Although I had to close FBC when Keith got out of the Navy and we moved back to our home state, I enjoyed helping people get on track with their finances.

Back home, unfortunately, we didn't always take care of money as we should have then. Keith sometimes worked two or three jobs at a time, but we never seemed to get ahead. We often didn't answer the phone to avoid bill collectors.

We bought a property in the country to avoid paying rent, something that we had longed for since early in our marriage. Then Keith got seriously hurt on his job. For two years, there was no income at all, a new mortgage, and three kids still at home. We explained our plight to banks and bill collectors while we waited for the company, surgeons, and lawyers to agree to compensate. When it finally came, the settlement only amounted to enough to pay off the bills that had piled up during the two-year wait.

I'd had enough. It was time, once again, to follow the money control steps that I had taught others.

Once we got back to the basics, we were able to get our mortgage and credit card debt paid off. We also paid off two vehicles, a side-by-side, and a camper. We are now retired and able to travel. I choose to work tax seasons to help families get their best refund and pay less tax.

We still live humbly, and time and changing needs have altered how we handle money. One thing hasn't changed.

We are now much wiser and more diligent in how we handle our finances. We budget.

My Motivation

The last few years have been very busy. While COVID may have stopped some in their tracks, we've been busy at home, realigning priorities. Lately, I've been feeling a real push to share about personal budgeting because it's a very important aspect of my life.

I was in a grocery store recently and overheard a young customer ask an also young cashier how to prepare a chuck roast. Yummmm...my favorite way to cook chuck roast is in the crock pot with potatoes, onions, and carrots.

The cashier shrugged her shoulders. "I'm not really sure. Never done one."

The mom that I am, I spoke up. I first asked if the young lady had a crock pot. When she said she did, I gave her step-by-step instructions on cooking that roast in a crock pot. It took all of about a minute.

Some things you know; some things you don't. If you don't know and you want to know, you learn. If you want to learn, you ask someone who's done it. Then you do it. Then you know.

There are a lot of things I don’t know, but some that I do.

I can:

- Crochet – I only know four stitches, but almost all crocheting is based on these four (I think), so I can usually follow a pattern and get the right outcome. It’s a hobby that I save for winter so I can watch TV and be covered with nice, warm yarn.
- Sew – I used to sew better than I do now because I made more clothes when my kids were little. Instead of sewing being a passion, it was a chore. But I can if needed.
- Cook – Since cooking is one of the necessary steps to eating, I've learned enough to be able to prepare the same fifteen or twenty meals regularly. I do experiment occasionally when in the mood to be creative, but cooking is not my passion, either. It's a chore.

The list could go on and on. I have some experience in a lot of different things, but there is one thing that I'm passionate about; how money affects our household budget.

Let me rephrase that. I'm passionate about controlling money – instead of letting it control me.

If you read my message long enough, you'll notice I say that over and over again. I don't want to let money control me. And I hate to see it when it's happening to someone else. Mostly, I focus on budgets.

Budgeting seems to be a bad word for a lot of people. They have a preconceived notion that budgeting is restricting. Or they might think that they have so many bills and only so much money that a budget is moot. Others believe that they have plenty and therefore have no need of controlling spending, that they can get what they want when they want.

I fit all of those descriptions at one time or another in my past. When I was single, I had a great job and could spend whatever I pleased, and did. After having a bunch of kiddos, we had so many bills to pay on military pay that we couldn't afford squat. We were even on food stamps. I didn't think a budget could help that. But once I learned that budgeting was not restricting, but freed up resources, time, and worry, I was convinced that budgeting was going to be a lifesaver for our family.

It wasn't easy. Yes, there are restrictions, but you quickly learn what you can and can't live without. Our horizons had to expand to compensate for a strapped budget. We found that Chuck-E-Cheese wasn't nearly as much fun as a day at the beach. We could live without a movie theatre date once a week, but we could rent a movie to watch after the kids went to bed. We learned lots of new skills to make gifts instead of buying them. I learned to cook healthier meals for seven hungry mouths and nobody starved.

In short, it was work, but it was work that was necessary to take care of a large family. The result, however, was much better than just stretching money. The result was a can-do attitude that has benefited our lives considerably.

So why am I telling you all this?

Easy peasy. I'm getting older. I still have plenty of knowledge to offer. I'm most interested in teaching young people how to deal with money, but open to helping any age or income get a handle on personal money management.

Things that we learned in school, like balancing a checkbook, are no longer taught in today's classrooms. Many young grocery shoppers have no idea how to compare the costs of generic and brand names. Money management is a skill that every household can use to its advantage, and current educational systems don't teach how to be financially healthy.

While everybody in the house doesn't have to have the same aptitude, what happens when your babies leave the nest? Are you still going to take care of their expenses for them? What happens if you lose your money-managing spouse, whether by death or divorce? Can you competently take over the financial reins and be confident? What happens if you are suddenly out of a job with no notice? Can you survive until your first paycheck on your next job?

That did happen to us, and you know what? We made it because we had trained ourselves in how to handle money issues.

It all started with a simple notebook. I can teach you what our friend taught us.

It's not a big book. I can't write pages and pages of fluff. That's not me.

If you want to learn important steps toward taking control of money in your house, no matter your income, marital status, your living arrangements, or your age, this book is for you. It's a step-by-step guide to controlling in-hand money.

I don't give investment advice, or tell you what to spend your money on. I teach you the budget system that I have been using successfully for many years. It's kind of a hybrid of several different systems, and none of the steps are hard to understand or put into practice. In fact, after reading this book, you can be on the road to financial recovery immediately.

STU'S LAMENT

Stu and Carol

Stu and Carol have plenty of income. Stu is a successful structural engineer and Carol has never had a job outside the home. Their children are grown and have given Stu and Carol six grandchildren. Carol spends on gifts for the grandchildren with her credit card as she pleases, while Stu, who handles the family finances, is often shocked at the size of her credit card bill each month. Carol loves to cook, so Stu planned to have their kitchen remodeled into Carol's dream kitchen, but he is concerned that Carol's lavish gifting will squash that surprise.

Mark is Stu's close friend. Stu is groaning over Carol's credit card bill.

> *Stu: Mark, man, I don't know what to do. You know I make enough money to do whatever. I've got something that I've wanted to do for Carol.*
>
> *Mark: You don't know if she'll like it?*
>
> *Stu: No, no, I think she'd love it! But, Carol spends on the grandkids like I have a gold mine! So I never*

know how bad her credit card bill is going to be from month to month. I want her to have her dream kitchen, but I don't know if I can afford grandkids, too. Heh, heh, that's a joke.

Mark: So you have a budget, right?

Stu: Of sorts. I keep a separate account for paying regular monthly bills, and the extra goes into a couple of savings accounts. Sometimes I have to use savings to pay off that credit card.

Mark: You know, we figured out a long time ago that we could control some of our spending if we budgeted everything. We earmarked all of our income for certain things, even dinner out or golfing. Once we spent what was earmarked for the month, we just told ourselves that if we wait a few days or a week, there would be funds to use for that again.

Stu: How did that work out?

Mark: Say I have $200 set aside for playing golf for the month. If I played every week, I used it up pretty fast. But by holding off one weekend a month, I didn't overspend, plus it gave me a weekend to take Laura out to breakfast. The extra benefit is that the *few dollars that are left are available to use for something else if needed.*

Stu: That seems kind of restricting. We have enough money to do whatever we want. She doesn't know about the kitchen remodeling plan and I don't want to tell her.

Mark: That could be a problem. Laura and I talk about all of our purchases that are over $100. There are three questions we ask each other. Do we want it? Do we need it? And can we afford it? We can generally afford what we want, but sometimes wants and needs get confused. That's why we talk about it. We decide if we need to spend the money now or if we can we wait and set the money aside to get it later. (Laughs.) And sometimes, we end up not buying after all. We've waited long enough that that instant gratification thing goes away.

Stu: I guess it's time to have that kind of discussion with Carol. I just don't know where to start.

HOW DO I START?

Stu realizes that he needs to do something about controlling finances, but doesn't know how to take the first step. How many times have you thought about managing money better and had no idea where to begin?

If you're like the rest of us, you've probably mulled it over several times but didn't take any action. You can think about doing something all day long, but if there is no action behind it, it's just thinking about it. And we all know that thinking about it doesn't get a job done. Even think tanks have to take some type of action, recording their thoughts and discussion, leading to a decision.

The first steps to setting up a budget are:

- Acknowledge that spending needs to be controlled.
- Decide to improve your financial situation.
- List pros, cons, and goals for budgeting.
- Commit to a minimum time frame or dollar goal.

Notice that each step listed here requires action.

Acknowledge

Are you happy with your financial situation? Money worries are one of the leading causes of stress. Forbes tells us that financial stress even leads to physical health problems[2]. Getting financially healthy removes that correlation. It's important, too, that if you are in a household with others, whether you are married or live with roommates, you discuss money issues and work at solutions together.

Stu doesn't want to tell Carol about the kitchen plans, but if Carol knew what he wanted to do, do you think she would agree to make some spending changes?

Decide

We've all had to do some decision-making at some time or another. Money management is no different.

Are you on the fence about being financially stable? Chances are, if you are reading this, you've already acknowledged an issue and decided to do something about it. Good for you! If you're still not sure if you can follow a budget, though, what do you have to lose? Decide to at least start the process. You'll find that being in control of your financial health is way easier than you think.

List

List the benefits of being in control of income and expenses. Then list the risks of living without money controls. Be sure to include physical and mental health as a benefit or risk.

You also need goals. Is your first goal to get out of debt? That is often what many people want. Maybe your goal is to save for a new appliance. Have you outgrown your home? How is your car holding up? List at least five financial goals, three short-term and two long-term goals.

Commit

Sometimes it's hard to create a good habit. Set yourself a goal to follow your decision for a certain length of time. Can you do this for three months? How about six months or a year? The great thing about this follow-through is that, as you experience positive results, you are inclined to extend the period or establish new goals as each one is met. Who knows? You might even decide to make budgeting and money control a permanent part of your lifestyle.

HOW DO I GET MY SUMMER VACATION?

Ron is a real estate broker. Ron and Martha have three school-age children, and Martha is the secretary where they attend school. They would like to go on summer vacations, but because Ron's income varies from month to month, they are afraid to spend money on what they consider to be a luxury.

Listen to Martha and her co-worker, Jane.

> *Martha: Jane, how do you do it? You and Fred have five kids and we only have three. Yet you guys go on trips for a couple of weeks every summer. I know Fred is in the insurance business, so he's probably on commission, too, right? Just like Ron?*
>
> *Jane: He is on a commission basis only, so you know how that works. You only get paid when you sell, although there is a bit each month when people pay their policy premiums.*
>
> *Martha: So how can you just take off and leave that business every year? Aren't you worried about*

there not being enough commissions coming in when you get back? How do you get through that? Is your paycheck enough to cover all your bills?

Jane: Basically, we budget for it. We've been on a budget for about three years now and we have an emergency fund set aside for just that. If commissions are down one month, whether it's because of the economy or if Fred just needs a break, we have funds to fall back on. We don't have to use it very often because we've learned a few things about controlling our money along the way, but it's calming to know that the money is there if we need it.

As for my paycheck, no, it doesn't cover everything. We need both of our paychecks to survive. But we don't worry because we have a plan.

Martha: But since he doesn't make the same amount every payday, how do you plan?

Jane: Here's the thing. We knew when Fred took the job that it was going to be a big adjustment financially. We decided right then that we needed to budget and plan for up and down times. And we decided that we were going to follow it faithfully for a year. We started tracking expenses, then set up the budget based on percentages. It works really well with variable income. We had to make a few adjustments after a couple of months, but, all-in-all, setting up a budget was the best financial decision we've ever made for our family.

Martha: You tracked all of your expenses before you set it up? Why did you do that?

SHOW ME MY MONEY!

Would you set out on a trip to someplace you've never been before without a map? I wouldn't either. If we want to get from Point A to Point B, we need to know where both Point A and Point B are.

While the overall financial status may be obvious, some of the details may be obscure until we dive deeper into our spending habits. That's why we track income and expenses BEFORE setting up a full budget.

Mapping Tools

You will need a couple of items for drawing your map. You can use an inexpensive subject notebook with enough pages for each category of spending to have a section. Alternatively, you could use an accounting ledger or a spreadsheet, or you might decide on budgeting software. You'll need a file folder, a shoebox, or a large envelope for depositing receipts until they are posted. You will also benefit from having a tiny pocket notebook to write notes when you're on the go or when receipts are not available.

It's pretty simple. Start today. For the next thirty days, remind yourself to get receipts for everything you spend, even if you have to write a reminder note. Whether the expense is a monthly bill, a snack from a vending machine, stocking up at the grocery store, or throwing change to the Salvation Army bucket, document every transaction. Eventually, when the cashier asks if you want your receipt, the automatic answer will be "Yes." In thirty days, this will be your habit.

If you don't get every single receipt when you make a purchase, don't worry. Just write yourself a note in your pocket notebook (so you don't have to try to remember it later) and put it with the rest of the receipts. You'll still have the information for posting later.

Your receipts and/or notes should include the date, store name, item purchased, the total paid, and the category of the expense.

Categorize Receipts

Money purchases the products and services we need in numerous categories. Some typical everyday expenses are listed in the next chapter. Notice that some items may fit into more than one category. For instance, if you list your home insurance under Housing expense, ALWAYS list it under Housing expense. The key here is to be consistent with how you categorize expenses.

Write the category of the transaction on each receipt. Some of you will find it easy to notate it as you get the receipt; others will wait until they get home and categorize it all at once. Still others will make the category decisions at the end of the day. You can use whichever process works best for you. Daily attention minimizes the chance of forgetting the details of the transaction.

You can break expenses down even further if you'd like more detail in specific areas. Under Housing expenses, you may separate Rent/Mortgage from Utilities, Insurance, or Maintenance. The more detailed your category breakdowns, the more precise the map is of your current position.

Post Receipts

No later than the end of your first week of receipt collection, post each day's receipts. Start by writing the Category at top of your notebook pages, a separate page for each. If you have more or fewer categories than we've listed, that's okay, as long as they are separated according to YOUR spending habits.

Post the information from each receipt to the proper category page, preferably in date order. This helps find transactions later if necessary. Be sure to include:

- Date
- Store Name
- Amount Paid
- Note or Memo (This is a short description of items purchased, i.e. groceries, school clothes for Johnny. This helps to locate transactions later, if necessary.)

Housing			
Date	Payee	Memo	Amount
12/31/2020	County Collector	taxes	$356.00
2/13/2021	Unity Bank	Mortgage	$871.32
2/19/2021	Pat's Glass	window repair	$140.00
3/13/2021	Unity Bank	Mortgage	$871.32

Posting Example

File the receipts. You may decide to file them in a monthly or a category folder. It's your decision. Some receipts don't necessarily have to be kept after posting, but if you make a major purchase or pay any bill that might be deductible on your tax return, KEEP YOUR RECEIPT. Also, be sure to keep receipts that show the payoff of any debt.

Tally Receipts

At the end of the first month, it's time to tally up those transactions. Add up expenses in each category. Use a blank page in your notebook or ledger to list Category totals for the month. This will give you a picture of how every penny worked for you for the entire month. Armed with this information, you'll be able to look at each category and decide where you can trim back spending and how to plan for occasional, major, or yearly expenses like birthdays, appliance purchases, or vacations.

Category	Spent
Recreation	$200.00
Clothing	$40.00
Savings	$1,000.00
Healthcare	$95.00
Personal	$30.00

You can use this information to set budget parameters after the first month of posting. However, I normally advise clients to follow these beginning processes for up to three months. One month will give you a fairly good picture of how you spend, whereas three months will give a better average. You alone can decide what you're comfortable with as far as timing. The more information about spending habits you have, the more accurate your budgeted projections will be.

What if I do everything online?

Many financial websites have the option to download transactions. One of the stumbling blocks to making only online purchases is...how do I track it?

It's not as difficult as it might seem.

When online purchases are completed, most retailers email a receipt showing all of the pertinent information that we track. This is where using a spreadsheet or other software comes in very handy. Simply copy and paste the information needed into the spreadsheet or program. If your software can import transactions, this is even better.

See Tools For the System for a Reusable Automated Yearly Tracker.

TELL ME SOMETHING I DON'T KNOW

Peggy, a single mom, works full-time evenings at a nearby Wal-Mart and gets child support for her two children, ages two and five. Her parents, who both work, watch the children during her shifts. Earning minimum wage, Peggy sees that caring for the children takes a toll on her mom and dad. Enid is a coworker.

> *Peggy: How in the world do you afford child care with this job, Enid? My parents take care of my kiddos so I can work.*
>
> *Enid: I budget myself pretty strictly.*
>
> *Peggy: But how do you do that? I'd like to figure out a way that my folks won't have to watch the kids. I mean, Mom and Dad both work full time AND take care of the kids. It's starting to get to them and I'd like to give them a break.*
>
> *Enid: I started by tracking all of my expenses by category for a month. Since I have the same expenses every month, it was pretty easy. When I finished tracking for a month, though, I noticed that I was spending a lot more on eating out than I was*

on groceries. Then I figured out what child care would cost me. I was pretty sure that I could handle the extra expense if I cut down on the restaurant bills. It's been working for a while now.

Peggy: I don't get the category thing. Do you mean you have to decide on a category for every little thing you spend? What if I buy a pack of gum or a soda? How do you categorize that stuff?

Enid: I have categories for groceries, miscellaneous, personal items, and a bunch of others. Gum and soda, for me, I would put in personal items. You could put it there, or in groceries, or any category you want. The main idea is to keep similar expenses together so you know what you're spending in each area. I'll send you a list of the categories I use, okay?

Peggy: That would be great!

CATEGORICALLY SPEAKING

Budget categories, though typical, may include unique listings. Many categories, though, are relatable to nearly everyone. Use or add according to your individual needs.

When setting budget parameters, allocations to each category are based on Net Income. This is the amount of a paycheck after taxes are deducted. If expenses like Health Insurance or Donations are deducted before you get your paycheck, they should be added back to the Net Income, and then deducted from categorized expenses.

For example, if you have a Net Income of $400 weekly in a four paycheck month, and $25 monthly is deducted for a 401K or other retirement savings, add $25 to your weekly Net Income. Then add $25 to Savings: Retirement each month. You'll then be able to calculate that you are saving 1.5% of your Net Income toward retirement.

$25/$1600= .015

Typical Budget Categories

- House
  - Rent/Mortgage Principal
  - Mortgage Interest
  - Homeowner/Renter Insurance
- Utilities
  - Electric
  - Water
  - Trash
  - Phone
    - Landline
    - Cell
- Auto
  - Car
    - Maintenance
    - Gas & Oil
    - Insurance
  - Truck
    - Maintenance
    - Gas & Oil
    - Insurance
- Food
  - Groceries
  - Restaurants
- Medical
  - Doctors, Dentist
  - Hospital
  - Veterinarian
- Child Care
- Insurance

- Life
- Health
- Car
- Homeowner/Renter
- Pet

- Entertainment
- Savings
    - Emergency
    - Christmas Fund
    - Vacation
    - Retirement
- Debt or Credit Card
- Miscellaneous

MAKE IT REAL

Trudy lives with her dad and stepmom and is a junior in college. She's a full-time student and works part-time at school in a work-study program. She wants to move into an apartment when she graduates with her Business Administration degree, but can't seem to save enough to even hope to make that a reality anytime soon. Trudy and Sally have several classes together.

> *Trudy: I'll be so glad when this semester is over. I need to get a full-time job so I can move out of my dad's house.*
>
> *Sally: Why do you want to move? Doesn't your dad pay for pretty much everything?*
>
> *Trudy: I'm done with being a burden on him. He has a life. He shouldn't have to take care of me now.*
>
> *Sally: So what's your plan?*
>
> *Trudy: Actually, I don't have one, other than getting another job. I know I just need to save a lot of money to be able to put deposits down on an apartment. And I have no idea what kind of*

expenses I'll have when I move. So, what does it cost you to live off-campus?

Sally: Honestly, I have no idea off the top of my head. I keep my budget on my computer so I don't have to try to remember every little piece of it. I do know that I'm almost out of debt, except for this term's school expenses. I track and categorize income and expenses. The next step is building my emergency fund. Anything I have left over in most categories I transfer to paying off debt. That's my biggest focus right now.

Trudy: Please, please, please. Show me how you did that!

Two Months Later

Sally: You're ready for me to teach you how to set up a budget?

Trudy: Yep. I've been tracking expenses as you told me to. How hard is it?

Sally: It's not that hard. It's just a matter of developing some habits and sticking to them. You've already got a head start by tracking as you have for the last couple of months.

Trudy: Okay, so what's next?

Sally: Let's look at your tracking pages.

Trudy: I tracked seven different categories. That's all I have right now. I know it will be different when I move, but that won't be for a while yet, about 18 months. I'd like to have $5000 in savings to be able to move.

Sally: How much do you have in Savings now?

Trudy: Only $1182.

Sally: And did you write down your debt list?

Trudy: The only debt I have is a loan from my dad for my car. I pay him $100 a month. I only owe him $600 now.

Sally: Here we go, then, Trudy. We'll give all of your income a purpose.

SPECIAL FUNDS

Let's talk about tithes. Many people are familiar with the word tithe or tithing but do not understand where it came from or why. They normally associate it with church donations.

I am a firm believer that tithing affects our financial health. I also believe that tithing is a very personal decision.

Historical Backdrop

The Bible says that Abraham gave the king/priest Melchizedek a tenth of the spoils of war. The Israelites gave 10% of their harvest to help the poor or needy. Malachi 3:10-12 says "Bring the full tithe into the storehouse, so that there may be food in my house, and thus put me to the test, says the Lord of hosts; see if I will not open the windows of heaven for you and pour down for you an overflowing blessing."

Some use that scripture verse to require folks to tithe, saying that they won't be blessed by God unless they give 10% to a church.

I disagree.

I do believe that God is especially pleased when we give to help others, regardless of what type of help. It could be time, money, clothing, food...anything. And while we are not necessarily looking for a reward for it in this life, I believe giving is a portal to receive blessings, whether physical, financial, or spiritual.

Other Opinions

If you want to learn more, there are numerous articles online about tithing, both pro, and con. But here's the thing. We should all be giving something to help others. As Dave Ramsey says,

> *While tithing 10% of your income is biblical, that doesn't mean you have to be a Christian to tithe. It also doesn't mean you're a bad Christian if you don't tithe. And guess what? God loves us when we give* and *when we don't give. In fact, 75% to 90% of those who go to church don't give a tithe.*
>
> *Here's another truth bomb: Tithing isn't a way to earn God's love—because* we already have it. *In Matthew 23:23, Jesus warns against focusing too much on the rules of tithing without paying attention to the more important things like justice, mercy and faithfulness.*

Bottom line? You should be giving in some way. But tithing is more of a spiritual topic than a financial one. It's not about the money—it's about the heart. It's about living with the attitude that we've been blessed to be a blessing.

2 Corinthians 9:7 (NIV) says, "Each of you should give what you have decided in your heart to give, not reluctantly or under compulsion, for God loves a cheerful giver."[3]

How Does Tithing Calculate?

It's up to you. You decide whether to tithe on your Gross Income or Net Income, or whether to tithe at all.

If tithing on all income, subtract it from your Gross Income to figure Net Income. If tithing on Net Income, set it up as a separate category to calculate as an expense. If you decide to give without tithing, you can set up Giving as an expense category.

I Have Debt!

Debt reduction is one of the main reasons people begin budgeting. When the credit card or loan payments get overwhelming, it's hard to make ends meet or have funds to supply the necessities of life; food, shelter, and clothing.

Having debt can often lead to more debt in the form of interest that is tacked on to the original purchase or loan. It can also affect credit scores, making it impossible to get a loan that is needed, for instance, to buy a home rather than rent. If we owe money to another, whether a company or an individual, it can be burdensome and even physically stressful.

Debt payments in a budget are regarded as an expense. There are several ways to handle debt payments, but the main premise is to get out of debt as soon as possible, relieving stress.

A favorite of many budgeters is the Debt Snowball. Minimum payments are made on all debts, with as much extra as possible being paid on the smallest debt. Once that one bill is paid off, the amounts previously paid on that bill are added to payment on the next smallest debt, until all debts are paid. It's a great feeling!

Another useful tool is the Debt Avalanche. Similar to the Debt Snowball, the highest interest debt is paid off first. That payment is then added to the debt with the next highest interest rate, and so on until all debts are paid. The advantage here is that higher interest charges will not build as quickly as they do with the Debt Snowball.

Using a separate page, list all debts. Include the name of the debt, the interest rate, the monthly payment, the number of remaining payments, and the current balance. Add up the monthly payments and total debt. These figures will be used later when setting up the monthly budget.

If you think you're too far in debt to see daylight, take heart. Thousands of others have budgeted themselves out of debt. YOU CAN, TOO!

Emergency Fund

Everyone needs it! We have all experienced some type of situation that can wreak havoc on a budget, no matter how diligent you are to control spending. A window gets broken while the kids are playing ball. A pet gets sick and needs treatment that costs more than the monthly pet expense allocation. The refrigerator stops cooling and needs to be replaced. These and hundreds of other situations can cause additional stress. Why? Because it takes money to fix them and there's not enough allocated monthly to handle the emergency.

Enter the Emergency Fund.

Emergency Funds should typically be the first savings account to be set up. The amount of the fund largely depends on your family size, income, and other savings. A minimum amount of $1,000 is generally recommended before starting any other savings account.

That doesn't mean stopping funding your IRA or 401K to save for emergencies. But, in an emergency, it might be possible to borrow from them. Check with your Human Resources department or your tax preparer to learn the current rules on borrowing from these accounts.

Once debts are paid off, a good practice is to increase the Emergency Fund to three to six times the monthly Gross Income. This gives some protection from big catastrophes, such as job loss. You never know when difficulties will arise and try to strike down the plans you've made.

PURPOSEFUL MONEY

Once tracking is completed and each category total is listed on an Income/Expense Report page (See Chapter 3), it's time to figure out percentages. Start by listing Monthly Income.

Gross Income	**$1000.00**
Deductions	$200.00
Net Income	**$800.00**

Using the Monthly Report Page, calculate the **% of Net Income** for each category.

Category	Spent	% of Net Income
Recreation	$200.00	25.00%
Clothing	$40.00	5.00%
Savings	$200.00	25.00%
Healthcare	$95.00	11.88%
Personal	$30.00	3.75%
Transportation	$129.00	16.13%
Food	$150.00	18.75%
Total	$844.00	105.50%

As you can see, Trudy spent $44 over her income for the month. She may have had money left over from the month before, or she might have taken money that she had previously saved to make up for the shortage.

Because she has only a car payment, that debt has been categorized as transportation. If there were many debtors, all debts would be combined into the Debt category.

These are the only categories that Trudy gave Sally to work with. Sally, however, showed guidelines for Trudy that included Donations. This budget is based on Trudy's $800 Net Income monthly. This is money that has a purpose: Purposeful Money.

Category	Budgeted	Allocation
Recreation	12.50%	$100.00
Clothing	4.00%	$32.00
Savings	20.00%	$160.00
Healthcare	12.00%	$96.00
Personal	4.00%	$32.00
Transportation	17.50%	$140.00
Food	20.00%	$160.00
Donations	10.00%	$80.00
Total	100.00%	$800.00

DRASTIC CHANGES?

Trudy: I like the idea that I can contribute to help others within this budget. So, basically, because I overspent my income, you're setting it up so that I don't spend as much in each category, but can still spend something, right? And still be able to give.

Sally: Yes, that's true. And keep these things in mind.

One, you said that during the summer, you plan to find a full-time job until school starts next term. That will increase your income a lot. You can still use the same percentages then, too. So if you make, say, $2400 per month, each allocation will be three times what it is now for those months you work full time. Since you won't need that much for expenses, you'll be able to put most of the increase into savings for your move.

Two, even if you don't get another job, as long as you don't take any out of your savings, you'll still have over $4000 for your move. Not quite at your goal, but if you find that you have excess in any *category for a particular month, you can move that extra money to savings.*

Three, when you get your dad paid off for the car in six months, you'll be able to apply that money to saving an Emergency fund.

And four, when you reach the savings goal for moving, you can start saving for whatever you want. The beauty of this system is that it is very flexible while helping you to control your money.

SOME THINGS GOTTA GO!

Knowing that she has overspent in the previous month, and because she is tracking expenses to stay within budget, Trudy will be more apt to curtail some of her discretionary spending. What to change in spending habits is a personal preference. Everyone will have a different approach as to what is and is not important to them.

Just because we have discretionary spending doesn't mean we have to spend it all right now. It depends on our goals. We've learned that there are many reasons to set a purpose in place.

Is It Worth It?

Think about Stu and his desire to give Carol her dream kitchen. What effect do you think it will have on Carol to know that if she controls her spending a little now, she'll have exactly the kitchen she's been hoping for sooner rather than later?

How about Ron and Martha? If they can manage their money a little better, they won't have to fear being without during lean real estate months. Having that

Emergency fund built up to cover six months will give them the freedom to take those summer vacations while their children are still home to enjoy them.

Peggy's concerns about her parents' well-being will never go away, but she will know that her children aren't the cause of any extra anxiety once she trims spending to be able to afford other child care.

The reasons to budget money are many, but the steps and the results, if followed, will always be the same: more freedom and less stress.

Do My Credit Cards Have To Go?

In a word, yes. Or, no. It all depends on you.

Why are you using credit cards? If you use credit cards to get through the month because you've run out of other funds, STOP. Put them in a drawer, or a safe, or a file cabinet, something. Get them out of your purse or wallet. You're using them wrong!

Of course, that's not what credit card companies will tell you. They want you to use them indiscriminately, spending more than you can pay off each month so that you will owe them more interest. That's a very expensive trap. Interest rates can be as high as 36%. Plus many cards charge an annual fee just for having the card.

Credit cards are surely the biggest money pit on the planet. Unless you use them right, that is.

Can You Ever Use A Credit Card Right?

Yes, you can!

Paying by credit card makes tracking spending a bit easier, but there are trade-offs that you may not want to make.

> *Fred: We have two cards that we rely on, not to get through the month, but to actually make money. And we have one as a backup for emergencies. But, since we now have an emergency fund, we rarely use it.*
>
> *The first is a cash-back card that pays us 1.5% for every single purchase. There is no fee through our credit union and we pay off the card before the due date each month. We use this card for almost every purchase, including monthly bills, groceries, and eating out.*
>
> *The second is also a cash-back card from Costco that pays us a minimum of 2% for Costco purchases, and up to 4% if we buy our gas at Costco. There is an annual fee for this card, but if we don't spend enough to pay for the yearly membership, they downgrade our membership and refund the fee. That hasn't happened in the three years we've had*

the card, and we've always received more cash than the membership fee.

To use or not use cards is a decision that only you can make. Are you disciplined enough to stay within budget? If so, a cash-back card can help grow your savings. If not, though, it's probably not a good idea to keep it handy. Take it out of your wallet or purse. Store it somewhere safe, to be used only in dire emergencies. Don't necessarily cancel it, though. If you cancel, it can affect your credit score.

It's important to research the options on every card that you would consider. Some free cards charge very high interest rates, which, if not paid off on time every month, can negatively affect your budget. Verify interest rates, balance transfer fees, annual fees, and late fees. If you're going to use a card, make it to your advantage.

IT'S NOT WRITTEN IN STONE

Trudy: So how will I know how to make changes when I get another job or when I graduate and move?

Sally: Making a little change is as simple as transferring funds from one category to another. You very rarely have to revamp all of your allocations. And adding income doesn't change how your funds are allocated. Revamping when you move, though, will mean adding categories and changing percentages.

One of the great things about this budgeting system is its flexibility. Do you find that you're not spending as much on clothing as you thought you needed? Maybe your kindergartner has graduated to elementary school and you no longer need daycare. Life is full of changes to our circumstances that warrant changes to our budget.

You might decide to save more toward vacation, or you might need to increase your grocery allocation to feed your teenagers. You might, like Trudy, be starting a new home. Very simply, if you no longer have expenses or you are regularly spending more in a particular category, or if you have new categories of monthly expenses, it's likely time to adjust your percentages.

But if your changes are temporary, only a month or two, for instance, it's very easy to transfer funds from one category, decreasing the balance available, to another category, giving you a little extra to spend.

Housing				
Date	Payee	Memo	Amount	Balance
2/13/2021	Unity Bank	Mortgage	$871.32	$423.68
2/19/2021	Pat's Glass	window repair	$140.00	$283.68
2/19/2021	Transfer to Food		$100.00	$183.68

Food				
Date	Payee	Memo	Amount	Balance
2/2/2021	Shop and Save	Groceries	$49.32	$150.68
2/8/2021	Costco	Groceries	$112.76	$37.92
2/8/2021	Shop and Save	Groceries	$21.09	$16.83
2/19/2021	Transfer from Housing		+$100.00	$116.83
2/19/2021	Shop and Save	Groceries	$61.41	$55.42

A Word Of Caution

It is ill-advised to rely on transferring funds from one category to another just to satisfy a whim. By all means, it's your money to do with as you wish. But if your goal is to control spending to reach certain financial milestones, overcome that desire for immediate gratification. Think about what's important. Do you need to spend now? Or is what you want worth saving for?

SOFTWARE, ETC.

Trudy: If I need to change everything, like when I move, how do I know how much to allocate to each category? Since my spending will be way different, I'll have no idea where to start.

Sally: Several websites list budget percentage guidelines for all different family sizes. That's where I go to get my information. I have a couple of sites that I compare and use what I think is best for me.[4]

There are hundreds of tools available online to make budgeting easier. Free and paid desktop software and mobile apps are all over the internet. Your bank may even have a budgeting app on its website. How you do your tracking and posting is a matter of preference.

My favorites are, unfortunately, only accessed online.

MoneyLife

Crown Financial Ministries offers MoneyLife. It is FREE! Find it at https://planner.crown.org/

To be honest, this is the program that we used for about twenty years, only when we started it was totally on paper. Besides being free, MoneyLife has a Daily Tracker, and a Detailed Budget Report, and helps with debt reduction with a Debt Snowball. As you initially set it up, MoneyLife asks questions to help you remember your expenses, and gives budgeting tips along the way.

MoneyLife is my number-one choice if you are using an online system.

YNAB

YNAB (https://www.youneedabudget.com/) was my go-to once I started tracking on my computer. YNAB allows you to import transactions from your bank. You can plan for occasional bills, and share data with your spouse/partner. You can easily see all of your accounts and transfer between them. Regular monthly payments can be scheduled. An online feature that they did not have when I used the program is goal-setting.

Even though I used YNAB religiously for tracking, though, it cannot allocate by percentage, which is my preference. I had to figure out percentages and allocations on my own. Also, some folks have had issues with the mobile app's "auto assign" feature.

When I first started using YNAB, it was a stand-alone program with a companion app. Now YNAB requires a paid subscription and is only cloud-based.

EveryDollar

You've probably heard of Dave Ramsey. Dave has an awesome app called EveryDollar (https://www.ramseysolutions.com/ramseyplus/everydollar/). You can set goals, track, and get reports on any device. You can also sync with your bank, and export transactions. The biggest advantage, in my opinion, is that you can set category percentages with EveryDollar, so if you have variable income, the percentage per paycheck will remain the same.

I have never used EveryDollar, but the screenshots look like this is a budgeter's dream, except for the price tag, as EveryDollar also requires a cloud-based paid subscription.

What I Do

I'm not a fan of posting all of my financial information online. Nobody else needs to know how we spend our money. Yes, I bank and pay my bills online, but who besides me needs a compilation of all of my accounts and spending? NOBODY!

I use spreadsheets on my computer that I have programmed and developed myself. By posting each transaction on their respective category pages each day, my reports are updated immediately. The downside is that I don't have a companion mobile app for viewing reports, but if I upload daily updates to Google docs, I can see the reports on my phone.

It’s not my favorite way to track and get reports, but I feel it is the best safeguard against identity theft in this current climate. Here is an example of the Year Report. Tracking sheet examples are in Chapter 3. You can also use a plain spiral notebook and handwrite your data. Again, use what you are comfortable with.

Year Report

2022

Gross	$72,000.00
Deductions	$8,400.00
Net Income	$63,840.00

Expenses	$33,876.00
Surplus	$37,645.60
Shortfall	($7,681.60)
YE Balance	$63,840.00

Category	Jan	Feb	Mar	Apr	May	Jun	Jul	Aug	Sep	Oct	Nov	Dec	Spent	% of Income	Budgeted %	Allocation	Surplus	Shortfall
Tithe	$646.00	$1,226.00	$646.00	$646.00	$646.00	$646.00	$646.00	$646.00	$646.00	$646.00	$646.00	$646.00	$8,332.00	13.05%	10.00%	$6,384.00	$0.00	$1,608.00
Taxes	$281.00	$281.00	$281.00	$281.00	$281.00	$281.00	$281.00	$281.00	$281.00	$281.00	$281.00	$281.00	$3,372.00	5.28%	14.50%	$9,256.80	$5,884.80	$0.00
Housing	$631.00	$631.00	$631.00	$631.00	$631.00	$631.00	$631.00	$631.00	$631.00	$631.00	$631.00	$25.00	$6,966.00	10.91%	15.00%	$9,576.00	$2,610.00	$0.00
Food	$181.00	$181.00	$181.00	$181.00	$181.00	$181.00	$181.00	$181.00	$181.00	$181.00	$181.00	$181.00	$2,172.00	3.40%	10.00%	$6,384.00	$4,212.00	$0.00
Transportation	$231.00	$231.00	$231.00	$21.00	$21.00	$21.00	$21.00	$21.00	$21.00	$21.00	$21.00	$21.00	$882.00	1.38%	30.00%	$19,152.00	$18,270.00	$0.00
Insurance	$320.00	$120.00	$120.00	$120.00	$120.00	$120.00	$120.00	$120.00	$120.00	$120.00	$120.00	$120.00	$1,640.00	2.57%	10.00%	$6,384.00	$4,744.00	$0.00
Debts	$0.00	$0.00	$0.00	$0.00	$0.00	$0.00	$0.00	$0.00	$0.00	$0.00	$0.00	$0.00	$0.00	0.00%	0.00%	$0.00	$0.00	$0.00
Recreation	$145.00	$145.00	$145.00	$145.00	$145.00	$145.00	$145.00	$145.00	$145.00	$145.00	$145.00	$145.00	$1,740.00	2.73%	3.00%	$1,915.20	$175.20	$0.00
Clothing	$20.00	$20.00	$20.00	$20.00	$20.00	$20.00	$20.00	$20.00	$20.00	$20.00	$20.00	$20.00	$240.00	0.38%	1.00%	$638.40	$398.40	$0.00
Savings	$160.00	$160.00	$160.00	$160.00	$160.00	$160.00	$160.00	$160.00	$160.00	$160.00	$160.00	$160.00	$1,920.00	3.01%	5.00%	$3,192.00	$1,272.00	$0.00
Healthcare	$231.00	$231.00	$231.00	$231.00	$231.00	$231.00	$231.00	$231.00	$231.00	$231.00	$231.00	$231.00	$2,772.00	4.34%	0.50%	$319.20	$0.00	$1,839.70
Personal	$20.00	$20.00	$20.00	$20.00	$20.00	$20.00	$20.00	$20.00	$20.00	$20.00	$20.00	$20.00	$240.00	0.38%	0.50%	$319.20	$79.20	$0.00
School	$20.00	$20.00	$20.00	$20.00	$20.00	$20.00	$20.00	$20.00	$20.00	$20.00	$20.00	$20.00	$240.00	0.38%	0.00%	$0.00	$0.00	$180.00
Gifts	$120.00	$120.00	$120.00	$120.00	$120.00	$120.00	$120.00	$120.00	$120.00	$120.00	$120.00	$120.00	$1,440.00	2.26%	0.50%	$319.20	$0.00	$840.70
Miscellaneous	$160.00	$160.00	$160.00	$160.00	$160.00	$160.00	$160.00	$160.00	$160.00	$160.00	$160.00	$160.00	$1,920.00	3.01%	0.00%	$0.00	$0.00	$1,440.00
New Category 1	$0.00	$0.00	$0.00	$0.00	$0.00	$0.00	$0.00	$0.00	$0.00	$0.00	$0.00	$0.00	$0.00	0.00%	0.00%	$0.00	$0.00	$0.00
New Category 2	$0.00	$0.00	$0.00	$0.00	$0.00	$0.00	$0.00	$0.00	$0.00	$0.00	$0.00	$0.00	$0.00	0.00%	0.00%	$0.00	$0.00	$0.00
New Category 3	$0.00	$0.00	$0.00	$0.00	$0.00	$0.00	$0.00	$0.00	$0.00	$0.00	$0.00	$0.00	$0.00	0.00%	0.00%	$0.00	$0.00	$0.00
New Category 4	$0.00	$0.00	$0.00	$0.00	$0.00	$0.00	$0.00	$0.00	$0.00	$0.00	$0.00	$0.00	$0.00	0.00%	0.00%	$0.00	$0.00	$0.00
New Category 5	$0.00	$0.00	$0.00	$0.00	$0.00	$0.00	$0.00	$0.00	$0.00	$0.00	$0.00	$0.00	$0.00	0.00%	0.00%	$0.00	$0.00	$0.00
Total	$3,166.00	$3,546.00	$2,966.00	$2,756.00	$2,756.00	$2,756.00	$2,756.00	$2,756.00	$2,756.00	$2,756.00	$2,756.00	$2,150.00	$33,876.00	53.06%	100.00%	$63,840.00	$37,645.60	$5,908.40

*Reconciliation: (Expenses) Plus (Surplus) Minus (Shortfall) = Net Income

WRAPPING IT UP

As mentioned before, seventy-three percent of Americans rank their finances as the number one stress in life, according to the 2019 Capital One CreditWise survey.[1] Forbes has documented the correlation between financial and physical health.[2]

If you have stress regarding finances, learn to budget. Learn to control every expense, have a purpose for your money, and stick to the purpose that you set. Good money management offers undeniable freedom. Knowing that physical and emotional stress about money can be reduced by tracking what you spend can be life-changing. This may sound a little simplistic but applies to nearly everyone.

What Do We Do With The Money We've Saved?

Remember Stu? He's going to build Carol's dream kitchen. Ron and Martha are finally going to take summers off with their kids. Peggy's giving her parents their freedom from constant babysitting. And Trudy is paying off her car and moving into her apartment.

Consider the goals that you set in the beginning. Did you want to get out of debt? Save for retirement or vacation?

Maybe you wanted to save college money for kids or grandkids.

Short-term goals should be reevaluated as you complete each milestone. The more short-term goals are reached, the closer you are to reaching long-term goals. Be realistic. While it may be entertaining to dream of owning the Taj Mahal, it will never happen. Dialing down to the attainable, though, can keep a dream alive until it becomes the truth.

Whatever your financial desires may be, focus on staying within budget to get the most for your money. Get out of debt. Save for your future. Prepare for emergencies.

What If I Fail?

You don't fail unless you quit. You may have setbacks. You may have time crunches that prevent you from keeping up with posting your data. But the only failure to budgeting is to not budget.

Don't give up. You have dreamed the dream of financial freedom. You can get there. Follow the steps, make adjustments, and try again. Work at it. Make saving a priority. In time, you'll have a success story to tell, too, and I can't wait to hear it.

YOU CAN DO THIS! READY, SET, GO!

Set Financial Goals

Track Spending

Allocate

Control Expenses

Save: Emergency, Retirement, Vacations, Etc.

Help Others

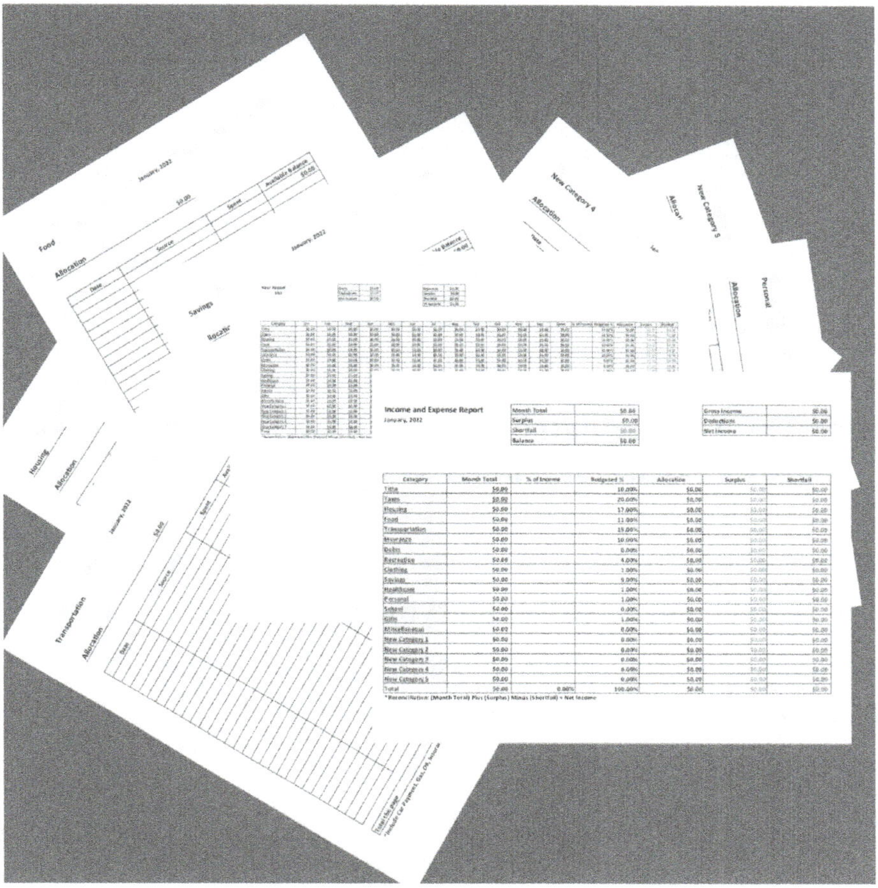

Budget Automation Package

Includes 20 category spreadsheets per month (12 sets)

Monthly Income and Expense Reports (12)

Yearly Report (1)

Instructions

ORDER TODAY! DOWNLOAD TODAY!

TOOLS FOR THE SYSTEM

As a thank-you for purchasing PURPOSEFUL MONEY, get 60% off Budget Automation Package, the spreadsheet system that I've developed to simply keep my budgeting data offline and updated. Normally $49, pay only $19.60 with your discount. Get immediate download.

To take advantage of this offer, type this address into your web browser. Note that you will need a spreadsheet application to use these sheets, i.e. Microsoft Excel, or Libre Office Calc (free)

https://unique-creator-3546.ck.page/products/yearwp?promo=9J73D19E96

- **Get the actual spreadsheets that I have developed for tracking a whole year's worth of income and expenses.**

- **Stay offline! Keep your private data on your own computer. No need to save to the cloud or someone else's server.**

- **Never purchase again! Just make a new copy of the folder each year. Use it forever with no future fee.**

- **Input each receipt only once to get a full report on how much you've spent in each category and the percentage of your income that you're spending in that category.**

- **Track monthly and yearly in one simple step.**

END NOTES

Crown Financial Ministries. "Spending Guides - Crown.Org." *Crown*, Crown Financial Ministries, 5 May 2017, https://www.crown.org/resources/spending-budget-guides/. Accessed 28 Nov. 2022.

Frazier, Liz. "Financial Wellness Is Critical to Your Overall Health - And Financial Literacy Is the Key." *Forbes*, 19 Jan. 2022, https://www.forbes.com/sites/lizfrazierpeck/2022/01/19/financial-wellness-is-critical-to-your-overall-healthand-financial-literacy-is-the-key/?sh=67c3670f2cdc. Accessed 28 Nov. 2022.

Solutions, Ramsey. "Tithes and Offerings: Your Questions Answered." *Ramsey Solutions*, 9 July 2021, https://www.ramseysolutions.com/budgeting/daves-advice-on-tithing-and-giving. Accessed 28 Nov. 2022.

White, Alexandria. "73% of Americans Rank Their Finances as the No. 1 Stress in Life, According to New Capital One CreditWise Survey." *CNBC*, 17 Oct. 2019, https://www.cnbc.com/select/73-percent-of-americans-rank-finances-as-the-number-one-stress-in-life/. Accessed 28 Nov. 2022.

Made in the USA
Monee, IL
17 January 2023

24520324R10039